RHYTHM PRIMER

by
Bruce Arnold

Muse Eek Publishing Company
New York, New York

ISBN-13: 978-1-890944-03-2

Printed in the United States

This publication can be purchased from your local bookstore, on-line via our shopping cart, or by
contacting:
Muse Eek Publishing Company
P.O. Box 509
New York, NY 10276, USA
Toll Free in USA: 866-415-8960
Phone: 212-473-7030
Fax: 212-473-4601
http://www.muse-eek.com
sales@muse-eek.com

Table Of Contents

Acknowledgments

The author would like to thank Michal Shapiro for proof reading and helpful suggestions. I would also like to thank my students who through their questions helped me to see their needs so that I might address them as best I could.

About the Author

Bruce Arnold is from Sioux Falls, South Dakota. His educational background started with 3 years of music study at the University of South Dakota; he then attended the Berklee College of Music where he received a Bachelor of Music degree in composition. During that time he also studied privately with Jerry Bergonzi and Charlie Banacos.

Mr. Arnold has taught at some of the most prestigious music schools in America, including the New England Conservatory of Music, Dartmouth College, Berklee College of Music, Princeton University and New York University. He is a performer, composer, jazz clinician and has an extensive private instruction practice.

Currently Mr. Arnold is performing with his own "The Bruce Arnold Trio," and "Eye Contact" with Harvie Swartz, as well as with two experimental bands, "Release the Hounds" a free improv group, and "Spooky Actions" which re-interprets the work of 20th Century classical masters.

His debut CD "Blue Eleven" (MMC 2036J) received great critical acclaim, and his most recent CD "A Few Dozen" was released in January 2000. The Los Angeles Times said of this release "Mr. Arnold deserves credit for his effort to expand the jazz palette."

For more information about Mr. Arnold check his website at http://www.arnoldjazz.com This website contains audio examples of Mr. Arnold's compositions and a workshop section with free downloadable music exercises.

Foreword

Many of my students have asked me how they can improve their comprehension and execution of rhythms. This book is an attempt to fill those needs.

Although there are many books out that help you learn your rhythms this series of books is unique in that each example is accompanied by an audio example. These audio examples can be downloaded for free from the internet at http://www.muse-eek.com. The audio files use midifiles which can be played on a Mac or IBM computer by using a midifileplayer or any sequencer program. Midifile players are available for free at many sites on the internet. muse-eek.com lists a few places to download this software.

This book is part of a sight reading series aimed at getting a student proficient at recognizing and playing rhythms. Other volumes in this series will introduce melodic shapes in different stylistic contexts. See the final pages of this book for a complete listing and description of current music related publications.

Muse Eek Publishing has created a website with a FAQ forum for all my books. If you have any questions about anything contained in this book feel free to contact me at FAQ@muse-eek.com and I will happy to post an answer to your question. My goal is to educate and help you reach a higher degree of musical ability.

Bruce Arnold
New York, New York

Introduction

Rhythm Primer is for any instrumentalist seeking to develop their understanding of rhythms. Beginning music students will find this book to be of particular interest because it starts with very simple rhythmic exercises and gradually moves on to more complex rhythms.

There are nine basic rhythmic patterns found in music. This volume concentrates on those nine basic rhythms through four metric levels. Although the technical explanation of the four metric levels is quite involved, the basic thing to understand is that they represent the common ways that music is notated for different styles. For example the exercises on pages 19 through 27 of Rhythm Primer are written in the metric level that funk and rock music are most often notated in. So to restate, to work effectively with this it's not as important to understand metric levels as it is to be aware of all the metric levels that you will find music written in, so you will be prepared. By reading through the Rhythm Primer you will be exposed to the most important metric levels commonly found in music.

This book uses rests and ties minimally so that the beginning student can concentrate on learning the basic nine rhythmic patterns. Further volumes of this Rhythm Series cover more complicated rhythms with rests and ties and various metric levels. See page xxiv for a complete list of all books in the Rhythm Series.

Understanding Rhythm Notation

     The rhythm in a piece of music is presented in overall units call "measures" These measures are further divided up into beats. (More on this in a moment) Example One shows you one "measure" of music. There are many different symbols in a measure of music. These symbols show how to play the music. To the far left there is always a clef sign. This tells the reader what pitch level the notes will be on the staff. The clef sign used here is the treble clef sign, therefore the 4 notes presented in this measure would be four middle C's. The next symbol is the time signature. This tells you how the measure will be divided rhythmically. In this case the time signature is 4/4. The top 4 tells you how many beats are in a measure. In this case the measure has 4 beats in it. The bottom 4 tells you what unit of measure will be used to show those 4 beats. In this case the 4 represents a quarter note. So this whole measure is divided up into 4 quarters and these 4 quarters are each represented by a note called a quarter note. A quarter note would be held for one beat. A line is placed at the end of each measure to show where the end of each measure is.

Example 1

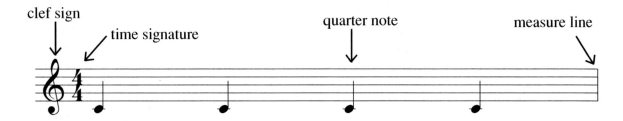

     Rhythm can of course be much more or less complicated than example 1. In example 2 we still have a 4/4 measure and it still has only 4 beats in the measure but we have only one note which happens on beat one. This note takes up all four beats of the measure so you would sustain the sound for four beats. This note is called a whole note. Example 3 shows a measure that has been divided up into two equal parts. These notes are called half notes and because we have a 4/4 measure there can only be 2 half notes in a measure because a half note gets 2 beats. The first note is played on beat one and the second note is played on beat 3.

Example 2

Example 3

As I have said, rhythm can be much more complicated than the previous example. In example 4 we still have a 4/4 measure and it still has only 4 beats in the measure but each beat has been divided into equal divisions to form a new rhythm. So now rather than just four rhythmic hits in the measure there are eight. These new notes are referred to as eighth notes because it takes 8 eighth notes to make up one measure of 4/4. So for each beat you would play two notes equally dividing that beat into two parts.

Example 4

Rhythm can be further subdivided. In example 5 each beat has been subdivided into three equal parts. These three note groups are commonly called triplets and usually have a bracket and a number three placed above the grouping. Therefore you would play three notes for each beat equally dividing that beat into three parts.

Example 5

We can also divide each beat into 4 equal parts. In example 6 each beat has been subdivided into four equal parts. Each note of this four note grouping is called a sixteenth note. Therefore you would play four notes for each beat, equally dividing that beat into four parts.

Example 6

We can also divide each beat into eight equal parts. In example 7 each beat has been subdivided into 8 equal parts. Each note of this eight note grouping is called a thirty second note. Therefore you would play eight notes for each beat equally dividing that beat into eight parts.

Example 7

Rests

Each of the rhythms presented in the previous seven examples could leave some notes out to create other rhythms. These left out notes are called rests and use the symbols shown below. During the rests you don't play anything. You will see in the forthcoming examples that when rests are placed into measures the rhythm can become quite complex. We will start with some simple examples.

Examples 8-10 show measures with three kinds of rests. In example 8 there is a whole note rest. Nothing would be played during this measure. Example 9 shows a half note rest. In this case nothing would be played for the first two beats of the measure. Example 10 shows a quarter note rest. In this case nothing would be played for beat 3 of this measure.

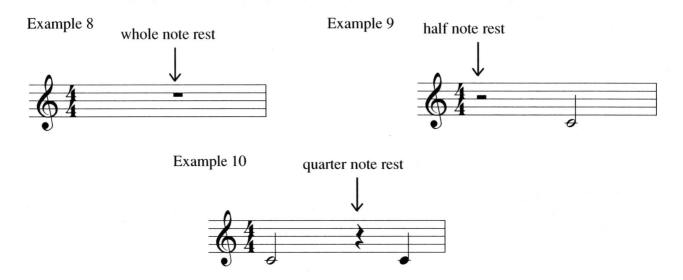

Examples 11-12 show measures that are composed of eighth notes but in which some of the eighth notes have been left out.

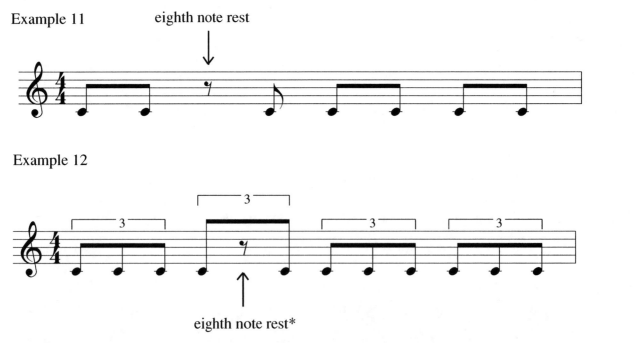

*Note: Eighth notes within a triplet receive 1/3 of a beat. Therefore when an eighth note rest is found within a triplet the eighth note rest equals 1/3 of a beat.

Example 13 shows you a sixteenth note rhythm where a sixteenth note rest has been added.

Example 13

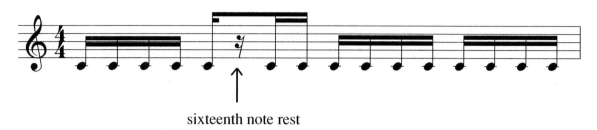

sixteenth note rest

Example 14 shows you a thirty second note rhythm where a thirty second note rest has been added.

Example 14

thirty second note rest

A measure can contain a variety of rests. Example 15 shows you a measure with various types of rests.

Example 15

* A sixteenth note is written with two *flags* on its right side to indicate its value when found alone.

Dots

A dot can be placed after a note or rest to lengthen its value. A dot adds 1/2 of the note's value, therefore in example 16, the dot placed after the eighth note rest adds a one sixteenth rest, totalling a rest of three sixteenths. (One eighth plus one sixteenth = 3 sixteenths.) Example 17 shows the same situation but with a note rather than a rest.

Example 16   dot   Example 17

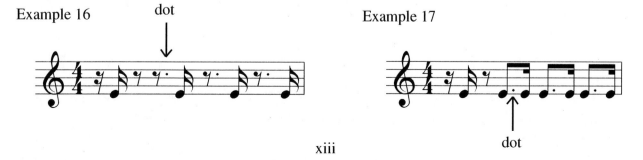

dot

Ties

Ties can also be placed into music to lengthen a particular note. Example 18 shows two quarter notes tied together. Example 19 shows what this rhythm would sound like.

Example 18

Example 19

Counting

Although I don't recommend it as a long term habit, a beginner often needs a method to help count each beat and subdivision. Over time you should develop the ability to recognize any rhythm and know what it sounds like. But again, if you are a beginner or you are having a problem with a rhythm, counting is a way to work it through. The follow examples give the counting method I recommend.

Understanding Triplets

Now that we have a basic understanding of how to read and understand rhythm let's take a more in-depth look at triplets. You will find triplet rhythms in almost every exercise in the Rhythm Primer book. It is important that you understand how to play these rhythms. If you are a beginner at music I would suggest you skip over the measures with triplets to begin with, and concentrate on mastering easier rhythms. You may find that listening to the midifiles found on the muse-eek.com website will help you to hear how the triplet rhythms sound.

The next pages deal with how to count and understand triplets. Make sure to listen to each example, because when you hear these triplets you will often find that the rhythm looks a lot harder than it really is.

Triplets divide a beat into three equal parts. In example 1, each beat has been subdivided into three equal parts. These three note groups are commonly called triplets and usually have a bracket and a number three placed above the grouping. Therefore you would play three notes for each beat equally dividing that beat into three parts. To play this example tap your right hand three times for each tap of your foot. Your right hand is playing the triplets and your foot is counting out the 4 beats of a 4/4 measure of music.

Example 1

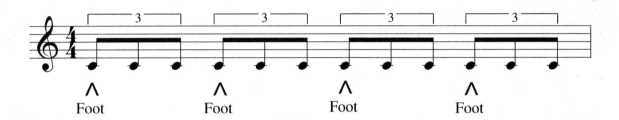

Although I don't recommend it as a long term habit, a beginner often needs a method for counting each beat and subdivision. Over time you should develop the ability to recognize any rhythm and know what it sounds like. But again, if you are a beginner or you are having a problem with a rhythm, counting is a way to work it through. Example 2 gives the counting method I recommend.

Example 2

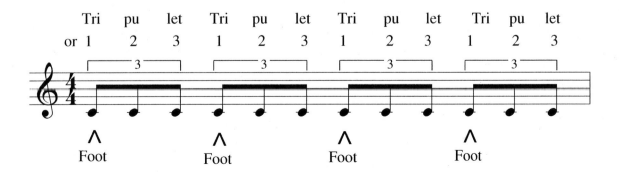

Triplets can also be found stretching over more than one beat. This can be very difficult for a beginning student to feel, especially when the tempo is slow. In example 3 we have two quarter note triplet patterns. Each quarter note triplet occupies two beats of the measure. These two beats are divided equally into three equal parts.

Example 3

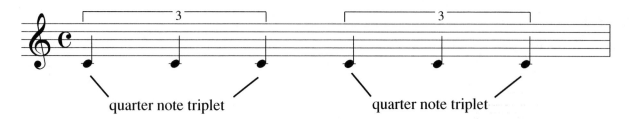

quarter note triplet   quarter note triplet

Sometimes it helps a beginning student to subdivide each beat in a measure in order to hear quarter note triplets. Example 4 is the same rhythm as example 3. The only difference is we have tied the notes of the triplet together in order to make it easier to see the rhythm. Many times writing a pattern in this manner helps a student to see exactly which notes are being played in the quarter note triplet. Notice the following aspects:

    a. The 1st note of the triplet in beat one is tied to the second,
    b. The 3rd note of the first triplet is tied to the 1st note of the triplet of beat 2
    c. The 2nd note of beat 2 is tied to the 3rd note of the triplet

This process repeats itself for beats 3 and 4.

Example 4

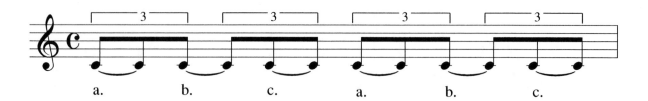

a.   b.   c.   a.   b.   c.

Example 5 shows you again the relationship between these two ways of writing quarter note triplets.

Example 5

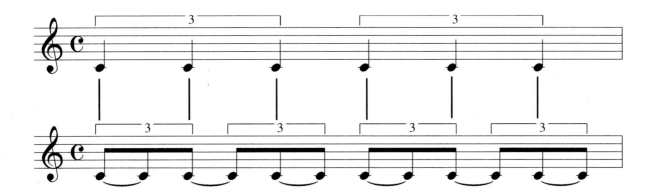

Playing this rhythm is a four step process.

1. Tap your foot on every beat
2. Tap your foot on each beat and say out loud each triplet as shown in example 2.
3. Tap the triplets with your right hand while continuing to do step one and two
4. Tap only the 1st and 3rd parts of the triplet in beat one and the 2nd part of the triplet in beat two while continuing to do step one and two.

You are now tapping quarter note triplets with your right hand. Continue this process so you can tap the quarter note triplets for beats 3 and 4 too. It will take some time before this is ingrained. I recommend doing this for 5 to 10 minutes a day for a couple of weeks and you should find that you are feeling quarter note triplets naturally.

Half note triplets are another rhythm commonly found in music. Half note triplets divide a 4/4 measure into 3 equal parts. Example 6 shows you a half note triplet.

Example 6

The same process of subdividing the measure will help you to see and feel a half note triplet. Example 7 is the same rhythm as example 6. The only difference is that we have tied the notes of the triplet together in order to make it easier to see the rhythm. Once again, writing a half note triplet in this manner will help you to see and feel the rhythm. Notice the following aspects:

a. The 1st note of the quarter note triplet is tied to the second.
b. The 3rd note of the first quarter note triplet is tied to the 1st note of the second quarter note triplet.
c. The 2nd note of the second quarter note triplet is tied to the 3rd note of the quarter note triplet.

Example 7

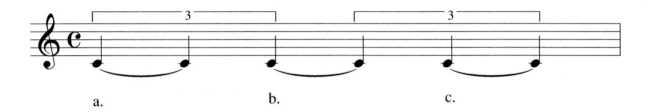

    a.   b.   c.

Example 8 shows you again the relationship between these two ways of writing a half note triplet.

Example 8

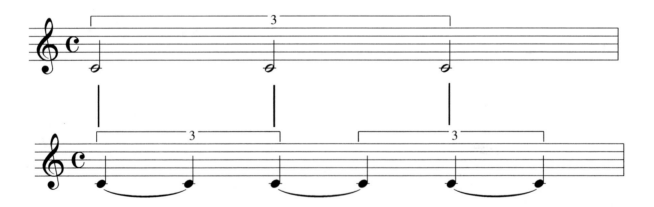

Once again this is a four step process in playing half note triplets.

1. Tap your foot on beats one and three of a 4/4 measure.
2. Tap your foot on beats one and three and say out loud each quarter note triplet as shown in example 9

Example 9

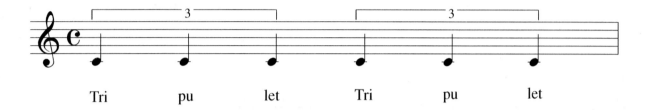

Tri   pu   let   Tri   pu   let

3. Tap the triplets with your right hand while continuing to do step one and two
4. Tap only the 1st and 3rd parts of the quarter note triplet in beat one and the 2nd part of the second quarter note triplet. Example 10 shows you the rhythm you are now tapping.

Example 10

      Now that you are tapping half note triplets with your right hand you should continue this process so you can tap the quarter note triplets for beats 3 and 4 too. Again, it will take some time before this is ingrained. I recommend doing this for 5 to 10 minutes a day for a couple of weeks and you should find you are feeling quarter note triplets naturally.

      Some interesting side notes to this process of learning triplets: Usually a student finds the faster they play triplets the easier they are to hear. This is particularly true of half note triplets where if you tap you foot once for a whole measure you only have to divide each tap of the foot into three equal beats with your hand or voice to create half note triplets. Experiment around with different tempos to help you feel triplets in many different ways.

Straight Eighth vs. Swing Eighth Note Feel

       Different styles of music interpret the written eighth note in various ways. Rock and Latin music in general play written music "as written," in other words you just play the notes as you see them.* On the other hand with a "swing feel" which is commonly found in jazz and blues, you play the eighth note with more of a triplet feel. If you have a measure of eighth notes as in (example 1) you would play these eighth notes like a triplet but leaving out the middle note. (See example 2.)

Example 1

Example 2

       * There are slight variations among all performers and styles as far as note interpretation goes. It should be kept in mind that examples 1 and 2 are only approximations of how eighth notes are played. Upon closer analysis you will find slight differences between any two styles of interpretation. It is recommended that you transcibe and learn melodies and solos of great jazz, rock and blues players to experience these differences first hand.

Assignments and Performance Directions for Rhythm Primer

The metronome markings found for each exercise are the typical speeds in which you will find music written for this metric level. **If you find any of the triplet patterns found in Rhythm Primer difficult, then first work through the following pages: 1, 3, 7, 8, 19, 20, 37, 38. Read the explanation of triplets found on pages 7-11 then work on all exercises with triplets. ***

Assignments and Performance Directions
Pages 1-6

Beginning Level:

Play each page at a slow tempo. Start at metronome = 60 for a quarter note. Work your way up to quarter note = 120. Do 3 pages a week. If you have problems understanding rhythmic notation or how to count rhythm see pages x-xiv.   See page xvii-xix for an explanation of the half note triplets found on pages 2, 4, 5, and 6.

Intermediate Level:

Play each page at half note = 60. The metronome should click on beats one and three. Work your way up to half note = 120. Do 3 pages a week.

Advanced Level:

Play each page at whole note = 60. The metronome should click only on beat one. Work your way up to whole note = 120. Do 3 pages a week.

Assignments and Performance Directions
Pages 7-18

Beginning Level:

Play each page at a slow tempo. Start at metronome = 60 for a quarter note. Work your way up to quarter note = 120. Do 3 pages a week.   If you have problems understanding rhythmic notation or how to count rhythm see pages x-xiv.

Intermediate Level:

Play each page at half note = 60. The metronome should click on beats one and three. Work your way up to half note = 120. Also try having the metronome click on beats two and four. Play both as a straight eighth feel and a swing feel.   See page xx for explanation of eighth vs. swing feels. Do 3 pages a week.

Advanced Level:

Play each page at whole note = 60. The metronome should click only on beat one. Work your way up to whole note = 120. Play both as a straight eighth feel and a swing feel . See page xx for explanation of eighth vs. swing feels. Do 3 pages a week.

* If you find triplets to be very hard I would recommend starting with pages 21-27 then 9-18 and then finally 2-6

Assignments and Performance Directions
Pages 19-27

Beginning Level:

   Play each page at a slow tempo. Start at metronome = 60 for a quarter note. Work your way up to quarter note = 120. Do 3 pages a week.   If you have problems understanding rhythmic notation or how to count rhythm see pages x-xiv.

Intermediate Level:

   Play each page at half note = 60. The metronome should click on beats one and three. Work your way up to half note = 120. Also try having the metronome click on beats two and four. Play both as a straight eighth feel and a swing feel.   See page xx for explanation of eighth vs. swing feels. Do 3 pages a week.

Advanced Level:

   Play each page at whole note = 60. The metronome should click only on beat one. Work your way up to whole note = 120. Play both as a straight eighth feel and a swing feel. See page xx for explanation of eighth vs. swing feels. Do 3 pages a week.

Assignments and Performance Directions
Pages 28-36

Beginning Level:

   Play each page at a slow tempo. Start at metronome = 60 for an eighth note. Work your way up to quarter note = 80. It is not recommended that you feel time in eighth notes when playing thirty second note rhythms. Beginners may find it useful to subdivide each beat until they feel more comfortable with reading thirty second note rhythms. Do one page a week.   If you have problems understanding rhythmic notation or how to count rhythm see pages x-xiv.

Intermediate Level:

   Play each page at quarter note = 40. Work your way up to quarter note = 50. Do one page a week.

Advanced Level:

   Play each page at quarter note = 50. Work your way up to quarter note = 60. Do one page a week.

Assignments and Performance Directions
Pages 37-45

Beginning Level:

Play each page at a slow tempo. Start at metronome = 60 for a quarter note. Work your way up to quarter note = 120. Do 3 pages a week. If you have problems understanding rhythmic notation or how to count rhythm see pages x-xiv.

Intermediate Level:

Play each page at half note = 60. The metronome should click on beats one and three. Work your way up to half note = 120. Also try having the metronome click on beats two and four. Play both as a straight eighth feel and a swing feel. See page xx for explanation of eighth vs. swing feels. Do 3 pages a week.

Advanced Level:

Play each page at whole note = 60. The metronome should click only on beat one. Work your way up to whole note = 120. Play both as a straight eighth feel and a swing feel. See page xx for explanation of eighth vs. swing feels. Do 3 pages a week.

Assignments and Performance Directions
Pages 46-61

Beginning Level:

Play each page at a slow tempo. Start at metronome = 60 for an eighth note. Work your way up to quarter note = 80. It is not recommended that you feel time in eighth notes when playing thirty second note rhythms. Do one page a week. Beginners may find it useful to subdivide each beat until they feel more comfortable with reading thirty second note rhythms. If you have problems understanding rhythmic notation or how to count rhythm see pages x-xiv.

Intermediate Level:

Play each page at quarter note = 40. Work your way up to quarter note = 50. Do one page a week.

Advanced Level:

Play each page at quarter note = 50. Work your way up to quarter note = 60. Do one page a week.

Rhythm Series

Below is a list of all the books in Mr. Arnold's Rhythm Series. By working through all these books a student will be well prepared for most commonly found rhythm patterns. All books include audio files for developing sharp rhythmic accuracy.

Rhythm Primer   ISBN # 1-890944-03-3
Rhythms Volume One   ISBN # 0-9648632-7-8
Rhythms Volume Two   ISBN # 0-9648632-8-6
Rhythms Volume Three   ISBN # 1-890944-04-1
Odd Meters Volume One   ISBN # 0-9648632-9-4
Contemporary Rhythms Volume One   ISBN # 1-890944-27-0
Contemporary Rhythms Volume Two   ISBN # 1-890944-28-9

It is also recommend that students use these books in conjunction with "A Big Metronome" ISBN # 1-90-044-37-8. "A Big Metronome" hones a student's natural internal clock, weaning them away from the steady click of a metronome. Advanced students will find this to be an excellent way to obtain the outstanding sense of time they wish to develop. See http://www.muse-eek.com for complete details on these books.

EXERCISE 1

EXERCISE 2

EXERCISE 3

3

EXERCISE 4

4

EXERCISE 5

EXERCISE 6

6

EXERCISE 7

EXERCISE 8

EXERCISE 9

9

EXERCISE 10

EXERCISE 11

EXERCISE 12

EXERCISE 13

EXERCISE 14

EXERCISE 15

15

EXERCISE 16

EXERCISE 17

EXERCISE 18

EXERCISE 19

EXERCISE 20

EXERCISE 21

EXERCISE 22

EXERCISE 23

EXERCISE 24

24

EXERCISE 25

EXERCISE 26

EXERCISE 27

EXERCISE 28

28

EXERCISE 29

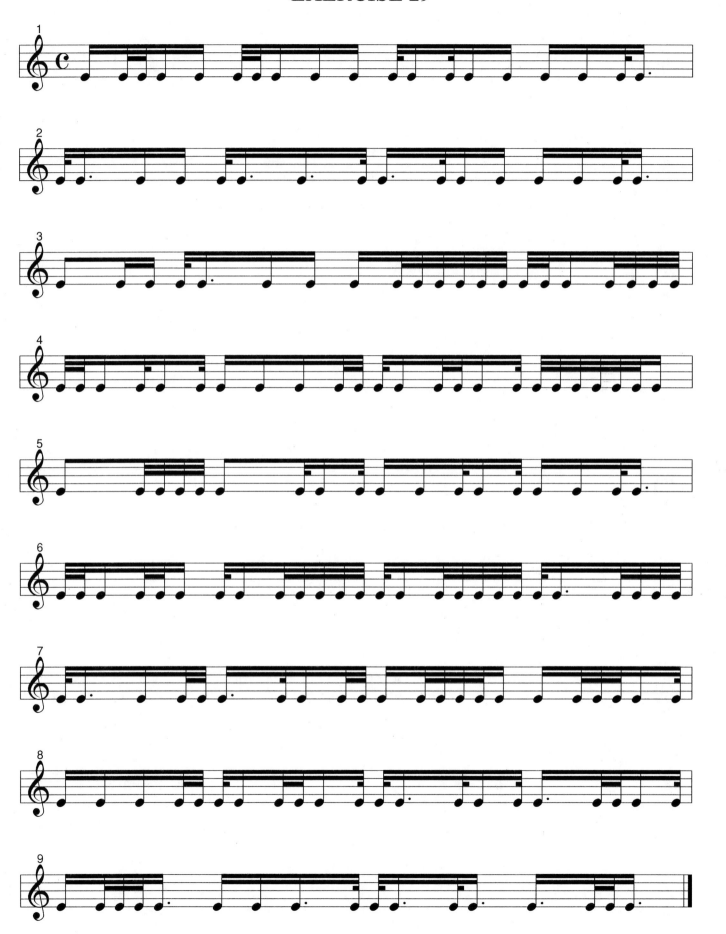

EXERCISE 30

30

EXERCISE 31

31

EXERCISE 32

32

EXERCISE 33

33

EXERCISE 34

EXERCISE 35

EXERCISE 36

EXERCISE 37

EXERCISE 38

EXERCISE 39

39

EXERCISE 40

EXERCISE 41

EXERCISE 42

EXERCISE 43

43

EXERCISE 44

EXERCISE 45

EXERCISE 46

46

EXERCISE 47

EXERCISE 48

EXERCISE 49

EXERCISE 50

EXERCISE 51

EXERCISE 52

EXERCISE 53

EXERCISE 54

EXERCISE 55

EXERCISE 56

EXERCISE 57

EXERCISE 58

EXERCISE 59

EXERCISE 60

EXERCISE 61

The Bruce Arnold series of instruction books for guitar are the result of 20 years of teaching. Mr. Arnold, who teaches at New York University and Princeton University has listened to the questions and problems of his students, and written forty books addressing the needs of the beginning to advanced student. Written in a direct, friendly and practical manner, each book is structured in such as way as to enable a student to understand, retain and apply musical information. In short, these books teach.

1st Steps for a Beginning Guitarist
Spiral Bound ISBN 1890944-90-4   Perfect Bound ISBN 1890944-93-9

"1st Steps for a Beginning Guitarist" is a comprehensive method for guitar students who have no prior musical training. Whether you are playing acoustic, electric or twelve-string guitar, this book will give you the information you need, and trouble shoot the various pitfalls that can hinder the self-taught musician. Includes pictures, videos and audio in the form of midifiles and mp3's.

Chord Workbook for Guitar Volume 1 (2nd edition)
Spiral Bound ISBN 0-9648632-1-9   Perfect Bound ISBN 1890944-50-5

A consistent seller, this book addresses the needs of the beginning through intermediate student. The beginning student will learn chords on the guitar, and a section is also included to help learn the basics of music theory. Progressions are provided to help the student apply these chords to common sequences. The more advanced student will find the reharmonization section to be an invaluable resource of harmonic choices. Information is given through musical notation as well as tablature.

Chord Workbook for Guitar Volume 2 (2nd edition)
Spiral Bound ISBN 0-9648632-3-5   Perfect Bound ISBN 1890944-51-3

This book is the Rosetta Stone of pop/jazz chords, and is geared to the intermediate to advanced student. These are the chords that any serious student bent on a musical career must know. Unlike other books which simply give examples of isolated chords, this unique book provides a comprehensive series of progressions and chord combinations which are immediately applicable to both composition and performance.

Music Theory Workbook for Guitar Series

The world's most popular instrument, the guitar, is not taught in our public schools. In addition, it is one of the hardest on which to learn the basics of music. As a result, it is frequently difficult for the serious guitarist to get a firm foundation in theory.

Theory Workbook for Guitar Volume 1
Spiral Bound ISBN 0-9648632-4-3   Perfect Bound ISBN 1890944-52-1

This book provides real hands-on application of intervals and chords. A theory section written in concise and easy to understand language prepares the student for all exercises. Worksheets are given that quiz a student about intervals and chord construction using staff notation and guitar tablature. Answers are supplied in the back of the book enabling a student to work without a teacher.

Theory Workbook for Guitar Volume 2
Spiral Bound ISBN 0-9648632-5-1   Perfect Bound ISBN 1890944-53-X

This book provides real hands-on application for 22 different scale types. A theory section written in concise and easy to understand language prepares the student for all exercises. Worksheets are given that quiz a student about scale construction using staff notation and guitar tablature. Answers are supplied in the back of the book enabling a student to work without a teacher. Audio files are also available on the muse-eek.com website to facilitate practice and improvisation with all the scales presented.

Rhythm Book Series

These books are a breakthrough in music instruction, using the internet as a teaching tool! Audio files of all the exercises are easily downloaded from the internet.

Rhythm Primer
Spiral Bound ISBN 0-890944-03-3   Perfect Bound ISBN 1890944-59-9

This 61 page book concentrates on all basic rhythms using four rhythmic levels. All examples use one pitch, allowing the student to focus completely on time and rhythm. All exercises can be downloaded from the internet to facilitate learning. See http://www.muse-eek.com for details

Rhythms Volume 1
Spiral Bound ISBN 0-9648632-7-8   Perfect Bound ISBN 1890944-55-6

This 120 page book concentrates on eighth note rhythms and is a thesaurus of rhythmic patterns. All examples use one pitch, allowing the student to focus completely on time and rhythm. All exercises can be downloaded from the internet to facilitate learning. See http://www.muse-eek.com for details.

Rhythms Volume 2
Spiral Bound ISBN 0-9648632-8-6   Perfect Bound ISBN 1890944-56-4

This volume concentrates on sixteenth note rhythms, and is a 108 page thesaurus of rhythmic patterns. All examples use one pitch, allowing the student to focus completely on time and rhythm. All exercises can be downloaded from the internet to facilitate learning. See http://www.muse-eek.com for details.

Rhythms Volume 3
Spiral Bound ISBN 0-890944-04-1   Perfect Bound ISBN 1890944-57-2

This volume concentrates on thirty second note rhythms, and is a 102 page thesaurus of rhythmic patterns. All examples use one pitch, allowing the student to focus completely on time and rhythm. All exercises can be downloaded from the internet to facilitate learning. See http://www.muse-eek.com for details.

Odd Meters Volume 1
Spiral Bound ISBN 0-9648632-9-4   Perfect Bound ISBN 1890944-58-0

This book applies both eighth and sixteenth note rhythms to odd meter combinations. All examples use one pitch, allowing the student to focus completely on time and rhythm. Exercises can be downloaded from the internet to facilitate learning. This 100 page book is an essential sight reading tool.
See http://www.muse-eek.com for details.

Contemporary Rhythms Volume 1
Spiral Bound ISBN 1-890944-27-0   Perfect Bound ISBN 1890944-84-X

This volume concentrates on eight note rhythms and is a thesaurus of rhythmic patterns. Each exercise uses one pitch which allows the student to focus completely on time and rhythm. Exercises use modern innovations common to twentieth century notation, thereby familiarizing the student with the most sophisticated systems likely to be encountered in the course of a musical career. All exercises can be downloaded from the internet to facilitate learning. See http://www.muse-eek.com for details.

Contemporary Rhythms Volume 2
Spiral Bound ISBN 1-890944-28-9   Perfect Bound ISBN 1890944-85-8

This volume concentrates on sixteenth note rhythms and is a thesaurus of rhythmic patterns. Each exercise uses one pitch which allows the student to focus completely on time and rhythm. Exercise use modern innovations common to twentieth century notation, thereby familiarizing the student with the most sophisticated systems likely to be encountered in the course of a musical career. All exercises can be downloaded from the internet to facilitate learning. See http://www.muse-eek.com for details.

Independence Volume 1
Spiral Bound ISBN 1-890944-00-9   Perfect Bound ISBN 1890944-83-1

This 51 page book is designed for pianists, stick and touchstyle guitarists, percussionists and anyone who wishes to develop the rhythmic independence of their hands. This volume concentrates on quarter, eighth and sixteenth note rhythms and is a thesaurus of rhythmic patterns. The exercises in this book gradually incorporate more and more complex rhythmic patterns making it an excellent tool for both the beginning and the advanced student.

Other Guitar Study Aids

Right Hand Technique for Guitar Volume 1
Spiral Bound ISBN 0-9648632-6-X   Perfect Bound ISBN 1890944-54-8

Here's a breakthrough in music instruction, using the internet as a teaching tool! This book gives a concise method for developing right hand technique on the guitar, one of the most overlooked and under-addressed aspects of learning the instrument. The simplest, most basic movements are used to build fatigue-free technique. Exercises can be downloaded from the internet to facilitate learning. See http://www.muse-eek.com for details.

Single String Studies Volume One
Spiral Bound ISBN 1-890944-01-7   Perfect Bound ISBN 1890944-62-9

This book is an excellent learning tool for both the beginner who has no experience reading music on the guitar, and the advanced student looking to improve their ledger line reading and general knowledge of each string of the guitar. Each exercise concentrates the students attention on one string at a time. This allows a familiarity to form between the written pitch and where it can be found on the guitar along with improving one's "feel" for jumping linearly across the fretboard. Exercises can be downloaded from the internet to facilitate learning. See http://www.muse-eek.com for details.

Single String Studies Volume Two
Spiral Bound ISBN 1-890944-05-X   Perfect Bound ISBN 1890944-64-5

This book is a continuation of Volume One, but using non-diatonic notes. Volume Two helps the intermediate and advanced student improve their ledger line reading and general knowledge of each string of the guitar. Each exercise concentrates the students attention on one string at a time. This allows a familiarity to form between the written pitch and where it can be found on the guitar along with improving one's "feel" for jumping linearly across the fretboard. Exercises can be downloaded from the internet to facilitate learning. See http://www.muse-eek.com for details.

Single String Studies Volume One (Bass Clef)
Spiral Bound ISBN 1-890944-02-5   Perfect Bound ISBN 1890944-63-7

This book is an excellent learning tool for both the beginner who has no experience reading music on the bass guitar, and the advanced student looking to improve their ledger line reading and general knowledge of each string of the bass. Each exercise concentrates a students attention of one string at a time. This allows a familiarity to form between the written pitch and where it can be found on the bass along with improving one's "feel" for jumping linearly across the fretboard. Exercises can be downloaded from the internet to facilitate learning. See http://www.muse-eek.com for details.

Single String Studies Volume Two (Bass Clef)
Spiral Bound ISBN 1-890944-06-8   Perfect Bound ISBN 1890944-65-3

This book is a continuation of Volume One, but using non-diatonic notes. Volume Two helps the intermediate and advanced student improve their ledger line reading and general knowledge of each string of the bass. Each exercise concentrates the students attention on one string at a time. This allows a familiarity to form between the written pitch and where it can be found on the bass along with improving one's "feel" for jumping linearly across the fretboard. Exercises can be downloaded from the internet to facilitate learning. See http://www.muse-eek.com for details.

Guitar Clinic
Spiral Bound ISBN 1-890944-45-9   Perfect Bound ISBN 1890944-86-6

Guitar Clinic" contains techniques and exercises Mr. Arnold uses in the clinics and workshops he teaches around the U.S.. Much of the material in this book is culled from Mr. Arnold's educational series, over thirty books in all. The student wishing to expand on his or her studies will find suggestions within the text as to which of Mr. Arnold's books will best serve their specific needs. Topics covered include: how to read music, sight reading, reading rhythms, music theory, chord and scale construction, modal sequencing, approach notes, reharmonization, bass and chord comping, and hexatonic scales.

Sight Singing and Ear Training Series

The world is full of ear training and sight reading books, so why do we need more?
This sight singing and ear training series uses a different method of teaching relative pitch sight singing and ear training. The success of this method has been remarkable. Along with a new method of ear training these books also use CDs and the internet as a teaching tool! Audio files of all the exercises are easily downloaded from the internet at www.muse-eek.com By combining interactive audio files with a new approach to ear training a student's progress is limited only by their willingness to practice!

A Fanatic's Guide to Ear Training and Sight Singing
Spiral Bound ISBN 1-890944-19-X   Perfect Bound ISBN 1890944-75-0

This book and CD present a method for developing good pitch recognition through sight singing. This method differs from the myriad of other sight singing books in that it develops the ability to identify and name all twelve pitches within a key center. Through this method a student gains the ability to identify sound based on it's relationship to a key and not the relationship of one note to another (i.e. interval training as commonly taught in many texts). All note groupings from one to six notes are presented giving the student a thesaurus of basic note combinations which develops sight singing and note recognition to a level unattainable before this Guide's existence.

Key Note Recognition
Spiral Bound ISBN 1-890944-30-0   Perfect Bound ISBN 1890944-77-7

This book and CD present a method for developing the ability to recognize the function of any note against a key. This method is a must for anyone who wishes to sound one note on an instrument or voice and instantly know what key a song is in. Through this method a student gains the ability to identify a sound based on its relationship to a key and not the relationship of one note to another (i.e. interval training as commonly taught in many texts). Key Center Recognition is a definite requirement before proceeding to two note ear training.

LINES Volume One: Sight Reading and Sight Singing Exercises
Spiral Bound ISBN 1-890944-09-2   Perfect Bound ISBN 1890944-76-9

This book can be used for many applications. It is an excellent source for easy half note melodies that a beginner can use to learn how to read music or for sight singing slightly chromatic lines. An intermediate or advanced student will find exercises for multi-voice reading. These exercises can also be used for multi-voice ear training. The book has the added benefit in that all exercises can be heard by downloading the audio files for each example. See http://www.muse-eek.com for details.

Ear Training ONE NOTE: Beginning Level
Spiral Bound ISBN 1-890944-12-2   Perfect Bound ISBN 1890944-66-1

This is a new method for developing instantaneous recognition of pitches within a key. This contextual-based ear training differs from interval based training by instilling a sense of key relationship; that is, a note is identified by it's characteristic sound within a key, and not by its distance from another note. This method has been used with great success and is now finally available on CD. There are three levels available depending on the student's ability. This beginning level is recommended for students who have little or no music training. A Complete Method book containing the Ear Training One Note Beginning, Intermediate and Advanced levels along with three accompanying CDs is also available for those students wishing to have a complete set of books and CDs under one cover.

Ear Training ONE NOTE: Intermediate Level
Spiral Bound ISBN 1-890944-13-0   Perfect Bound ISBN 1890944-67-X

This is a new method for developing instantaneous recognition of pitches within a key. This contextual-based ear training differs from interval based training by instilling a sense of key relationship; that is, a note is identified by it's characteristic sound within a key, and not by its distance from another note. This method has been used with great success and is now finally available on CD. There are three levels available depending on the student's ability. This intermediate level is recommended for students who have had some music training but still find their skills need more development.   A Complete Method book containing the Ear Training One Note Beginning, Intermediate and Advanced levels along with three accompanying CDs is also available for those students wishing to have a complete set of books and CDs under one cover.

Ear Training ONE NOTE: Advanced Level
Spiral Bound ISBN 1-890944-14-9   Perfect Bound ISBN 1890944-68-8

This is a new method for developing instantaneous recognition of pitches within a key. This contextual-based ear training differs from interval based training by instilling a sense of key relationship; that is, a note is identified by it's characteristic sound within a key, and not by its distance from another note. This method has been used with great success and is now finally available on CD. There are three levels available depending on the student's ability. This advanced level is recommended for advanced music students or those who have worked with the intermediate level and now wish to perfect their skills. A Complete Method book containing the Ear Training One Note Beginning, Intermediate and Advanced levels along with three accompanying CDs is also available for those students wishing to have a complete set of books and CDs under one cover.

Ear Training ONE NOTE: Complete Method
Spiral Bound ISBN 1-890944-47-5   Perfect Bound ISBN 1890944-48-3

This is a new method for developing instantaneous recognition of pitches within a key. This contextual-based ear training differs from interval based training by instilling a sense of key relationship; that is, a note is identified by it's characteristic sound within a key, and not by its distance from another note. This Complete Method book contains the Ear Training One Note Beginning, Intermediate and Advanced levels along with three accompanying CDsand is available for those students who wish to have a complete set of books and CDs under one cover.

Ear Training TWO NOTE: Beginning Level Volume One
Spiral Bound ISBN 1-890944-31-9   Perfect Bound ISBN 1890944-69-6

This Book and Audio CD continues the method of developing relative pitch ear training as set forth in the "Ear Training, One Note" series. There are six volumes in the beginning level series. Through practice, the student eventually gains the ability to recognize the key and the names of any two notes played simultaneously. Volume One concentrates on 5ths. Prerequisite: a strong grasp of the One Note method.

Ear Training TWO NOTE: Beginning Level Volume Two
Spiral Bound ISBN 1-890944-32-7   Perfect Bound ISBN 1890944-70-X

This Book and Audio CD continues the method of developing relative pitch ear training as set forth in the "Ear Training, One Note" series. There are six volumes in the beginning level series. Through practice, the student eventually gains the ability to recognize the key and the names of any two notes played simultaneously. Volume Two concentrates on 3rds. Prerequisite: a strong grasp of the One Note method.

Ear Training TWO NOTE: Beginning Level Volume Three
Spiral Bound ISBN 1-890944-33-5   Perfect Bound ISBN 1890944-71-8

This Book and Audio CD continues the method of developing relative pitch ear training as set forth in the "Ear Training, One Note" series. There are six volumes in the beginning level series. Through practice, the student eventually gains the ability to recognize the key and the names of any two notes played simultaneously. Volume Three concentrates on 6ths. Prerequisite: a strong grasp of the One Note method.

Ear Training TWO NOTE: Beginning Level Volume Four
Spiral Bound ISBN 1-890944-34-3   Perfect Bound ISBN 1890944-72-6

This Book and Audio CD continues the method of developing relative pitch ear training as set forth in the "Ear Training, One Note" series. There are six volumes in the beginning level series. Through practice, the student eventually gains the ability to recognize the key and the names of any two notes played simultaneously. Volume Four concentrates on 4ths. Prerequisite: a strong grasp of the One Note method.

Ear Training TWO NOTE: Beginning Level Volume Five
Spiral Bound ISBN 1-890944-35-1   Perfect Bound ISBN 1890944-73-4

This Book and Audio CD continues the method of developing relative pitch ear training as set forth in the "Ear Training, One Note" series. There are six volumes in the beginning level series. Through practice, the student eventually gains the ability to recognize the key and the names of any two notes played simultaneously. Volume Five concentrates on 2nds. Prerequisite: a strong grasp of the One Note method.

Ear Training TWO NOTE: Beginning Level Volume Six
Spiral Bound ISBN 1-890944-36-X   Perfect Bound ISBN 1890944-74-2

This Book and Audio CD continues the method of developing relative pitch ear training as set forth in the "Ear Training, One Note" series. There are six volumes in the beginning level series. Through practice, the student eventually gains the ability to recognize the key and the names of any two notes played simultaneously. Volume Six concentrates on 7ths. Prerequisite: a strong grasp of the One Note method.

Comping Styles Series

This series is built on the progressions found in Chord Workbook Volume One. Each book covers a specific style of music and presents exercises to help a guitarist, bassist or drummer master that style. Audio CDs are also available so a student can play along with each example and really get "into the groove."

Comping Styles for the Guitar Volume Two FUNK
Spiral Bound ISBN 1-890944-07-6   Perfect Bound ISBN 1890944-60-2

This volume teaches a student how to play guitar or piano in a funk style. 36 Progressions are presented: 12 keys of a Major and Minor Blues plus 12 keys of Rhythm Changes A different groove is presented for each exercise giving the student a wide range of funk rhythms to master.   An Audio CD is also included so a student can play along with each example and really get "into the groove." The audio CD contains "trio" versions of each exercise with Guitar, Bass and Drums.

Comping Styles for the Bass Volume Two FUNK
Spiral Bound ISBN 1-890944-08-4   Perfect Bound ISBN 1890944-61-0

This volume teaches a student how to play bass in a funk style. 36 Progressions are presented: 12 keys of a Major and Minor Blues plus 12 keys of Rhythm Changes A different groove is presented for each exercise giving the student a wide range of funk rhythms to master.   An Audio CD is also included so a student can play along with each example and really get "into the groove." The audio CD contains "trio" versions of each exercise with Guitar, Bass and Drums.

Bass Lines: Learning and Understanding the Jazz-Blues Bass Line
Spiral Bound ISBN 1-890944-94-7   Perfect Bound ISBN 1890944-95-5

This book covers the basics of bass line construction. A theoretical guide to building bass lines is presented along with 36 chord progressions utilizing the twelve keys of a Major and Minor Blues, plus twelve keys of Rhythm Changes. A reharmonization section is also provided which demonstrates how to reharmonize a chord progression on the spot.

Time Series

The Doing Time series presents a method for contacting, developing and relying on your internal time sense: This series is an excellent source for any musician who is serious about developing strong internal sense of time. This is particularly useful in any kind of music where the rhythms and time signatures may be very complex or free, and there is no conductor.

THE BIG METRONOME
Spiral Bound ISBN 1-890944-37-8   Perfect Bound ISBN 1890944-82-3

The Big Metronome is designed to help you develop a better internal sense of time. This is accomplished by requiring you to "feel time" rather than having you rely on the steady click of a metronome. The idea is to slowly wean yourself away from an external device and rely on your internal/natural sense of time. The exercises presented work in conjunction with the three CDs that accompany this book. CD 1 presents the first 13 settings from a traditional metronome 40-66; the second CD contains metronome markings 69-116, and the third CD contains metronome markings 120-208. The first CD gives you a 2 bar count off and a click every measure, the second CD gives you a 2 bar count off and a click every 2 measures, the 3rd CD gives you a 2 bar count off and a click every 4 measures. By presenting all common metronome markings a student can use these 3 CDs as a replacement for a traditional metronome.

Doing Time with the Blues Volume One:
Spiral Bound ISBN 1-890944-17-3   Perfect Bound ISBN 1890944-78-5

The book and CD presents a method for gaining an internal sense of time thereby eliminating dependence on a metronome. The book presents the basic concept for developing good time and also includes exercises that can be practiced with the CD. The CD provides eight 8 minute tracks at different tempos in which the time is delineated every 2 bars, and with an extra hit every 12 bars to outline the blues form. The student may then use the exercises presented in the book to gain control of their execution or improvise to gain control of their ideas using this bare minimum of time delineation.

Doing Time with the Blues Volume Two:
Spiral Bound ISBN 1-890944-18-1   Perfect Bound ISBN 1890944-79-3

This is the 2nd volume of a four volume series which presents a method for developing a musician's internal sense of time, thereby eliminating dependence on a metronome. This 2nd volume presents different exercises which further the development of this time sense. This 2nd volume begins to test even a professional level player's ability. The CD provides eight 8 minute tracks at different tempos in which the time is delineated every 4 bars with an extra hit every 12 bars to outline the blues form.   New exercises are also included that can be practiced with the CD. This series is an excellent source for any musician who is serious about developing an internal sense of time.

Doing Time with 32 bars Volume One:
Spiral Bound ISBN 1-890944-22-X   Perfect Bound ISBN 1890944-80-7

The book and CD presents a method for gaining an internal sense of time thereby eliminating dependence on a metronome. The book presents the basic concept for developing good time and also includes exercises that can be practiced with the CD. The CD provides eight 8 minute tracks at different tempos in which the time is delineated every 2 bars, with an extra hit every 32 to outline the 32 bar form. The student may then use the exercises presented in the book to gain control of their execution or improvise to gain control of their ideas using this bare minimum of time delineation.

Doing Time with 32 bars Volume Two:
Spiral Bound ISBN 1-890944-23-8   Perfect Bound ISBN 1890944-81-5

This is the 2nd volume of a four volume series which presents a method for developing a musician's internal sense of time, thereby eliminating dependence on a metronome.. This 2nd volume presents different exercises which further the development of this time sense. This 2nd volume begins to test even a professional level player's ability. The CD provides eight 8 minute tracks at different tempos in which the time is delineated every 4 bars with an extra hit every 32 bars to outline the 32 bar form.   New exercises are also included that can be practiced with the CD. This series is an excellent source for any musician who is serious about developing an internal sense of time.

Other Workbooks

Music Theory Workbook for All Instruments, Volume 1: Interval and Chord Construction
Spiral Bound ISBN 1890944-92-0   Perfect Bound ISBN 1890944-46-7

This book provides real hands-on application of intervals and chords. A theory section written in concise and easy to understand language prepares the student for all exercises. Worksheets are given that quiz a student about intervals and chord construction using staff notation. Answers are supplied in the back of the book enabling a student to work without a teacher.

E-Books

The Bruce Arnold series of instructional E-books is for the student who wishes to target specific areas of study that are of particular interest. Many of these books are excerpted from other larger texts. The excerpted source is listed for each book. These books are available on-line at www.muse-eek.com as well as at many e-tailers throughout the internet. These books can also be purchased in the traditional book binding format. (See the ISBN number for proper format)

Chord Velocity: Volume One, Learning to switch between chords quickly
E-book ISBN 1-890944-88-2   Traditional Book Binding ISBN 1-890944-97-1

The first hurdle a beginning guitarist encounters is difficulty in switching between chords quickly enough to make a chord progression sound like music. This book provides exercises that help a student gradually increase the speed with which they change chords. Special free audio files are also available on the muse-eek.com website to make practice more productive and fun. With a few weeks, remarkable improvement by can be achieved using this method. This book is excerpted from "1st Steps for a Beginning Guitarist Volume One."

Guitar Technique: Volume One, Learning the basics to fast, clean, accurate and fluid performance skills.
E-book ISBN 1-890944-91-2   Traditional Book Binding ISBN 1-890944-99-8

This book is for both the beginning guitarist or the more experienced guitarist who wishes to improve their technique. All aspects of the physical act of playing the guitar are covered, from how to hold a guitar to the specific way each hand is involved in the playing process. Pictures and videos are provided to help clarify each technique. These pictures and videos are either contained in the book or can be downloaded at www.muse-eek.com This book is excerpted from "1st Steps for a Beginning Guitarist Volume One."

Accompaniment: Volume One, Learning to Play Bass and Chords Simultaneously
E-book ISBN 1-890944-87-4   Traditional Book Binding ISBN 1-890944-96-3

The techniques found within this book are an excellent resource for creating and understanding how to play bass and chords simultaneously in a jazz or blues style. Special attention is paid to understanding how this technique is created, thereby enabling the student to recreate this style with other pieces of music. This book is excerpted from the book "Guitar Clinic."

Beginning Rhythm Studies: Volume One, Learning the basics of reading rhythm and playing in time.
E-book ISBN 1-890944-89-0   Traditional Book Binding 1-890944-98-X

This book covers the basics for anyone wishing to understand or improve their rhythmic abilities. Simple language is used to show the student how to read and play rhythm. Exercises are presented which can accelerate the learning process. Audio examples in the form of midifiles are available on the muse-eek.com website to facilitate learning the correct rhythm in time. This book is excerpted from the book "Rhythm Primer."